FRAGILE AND CONFLICT-AFFECTED SITUATIONS, SMALL ISLAND DEVELOPING STATES, AND EMERGENCY SITUATIONS
TECHNICAL GUIDANCE NOTE ON FINANCIAL MANAGEMENT

NOVEMBER 2023

ASIAN DEVELOPMENT BANK

 Creative Commons Attribution 3.0 IGO license (CC BY 3.0 IGO)

© 2023 Asian Development Bank
6 ADB Avenue, Mandaluyong City, 1550 Metro Manila, Philippines
Tel +63 2 8632 4444; Fax +63 2 8636 2444
www.adb.org

Some rights reserved. Published in 2023.

ISBN 978-92-9270-494-0 (print), 978-92-9270-495-7 (electronic), 978-92-9270-496-4 (e-book)
Publication Stock No. TIM230569-2
DOI: http://dx.doi.org/10.22617/TIM230569-2

The views expressed in this publication are those of the authors and do not necessarily reflect the views and policies of the Asian Development Bank (ADB) or its Board of Governors or the governments they represent.

ADB does not guarantee the accuracy of the data included in this publication and accepts no responsibility for any consequence of their use. The mention of specific companies or products of manufacturers does not imply that they are endorsed or recommended by ADB in preference to others of a similar nature that are not mentioned.

By making any designation of or reference to a particular territory or geographic area, or by using the term "country" in this publication, ADB does not intend to make any judgments as to the legal or other status of any territory or area.

This publication is available under the Creative Commons Attribution 3.0 IGO license (CC BY 3.0 IGO) https://creativecommons.org/licenses/by/3.0/igo/. By using the content of this publication, you agree to be bound by the terms of this license. For attribution, translations, adaptations, and permissions, please read the provisions and terms of use at https://www.adb.org/terms-use#openaccess.

This CC license does not apply to non-ADB copyright materials in this publication. If the material is attributed to another source, please contact the copyright owner or publisher of that source for permission to reproduce it. ADB cannot be held liable for any claims that arise as a result of your use of the material.

Please contact pubsmarketing@adb.org if you have questions or comments with respect to content, or if you wish to obtain copyright permission for your intended use that does not fall within these terms, or for permission to use the ADB logo.

Corrigenda to ADB publications may be found at http://www.adb.org/publications/corrigenda.

Note:
In this publication, "$" refers to United States dollars.

Cover design by Josef Ilumin.

 Printed on recycled paper

Contents

Table and Figures	iv
About This Publication	v
Acknowledgments	vii
Abbreviations	viii
Executive Summary	ix
I. Introduction	1
II. Financial Management for FCAS, SIDS, and Emergency Situations	5
Appendix: Illustrative Examples from FCAS and SIDS Contexts	14

Table and Figures

Table

ADB Financial Management Guidance Materials   2

Figures

1   The Project Cycle   3
2   The FCAS and SIDS Approach   4

About This Publication

This guidance note is issued by the Procurement, Portfolio and Financial Management Department of the Asian Development Bank (ADB) to guide ADB staff, consultants, and staff of executing and implementing agencies in performing financial due diligence and monitoring projects in the context of fragile and conflict-affected situations, small island developing states, and emergency situations.

The following is a list of guidance materials on financial due diligence issued by Procurement, Portfolio and Financial Management Department, showing the phases in the ADB project cycle to which they apply.

	Year Issued/ Updated	Processing			Implementation	Project Closing
		Concept Stage	Fact-Finding	RRP	Reporting	PCR
Financial Management Guidance on FCAS, SIDS, and Emergency Situations	2023	✓	✓	✓	✓	✓
Financial Reporting and Auditing	2022	✓	✓	✓	✓	✓
Cost Estimation in Sovereign Operations	2022	✓	✓	✓	✓	✓
Financial Analysis and Evaluation	2019	✓	✓	✓	✓	✓
Financial Due Diligence for Financial Intermediaries	2018	✓	✓	✓	✗	✗
Financial Management Assessment	2015	✓	✓	✓	✗	✗
Guidance on Using the APFS Checklist	2015	✗	✗	✗	✓	✓

APFS = audited project financial statement, FCAS = fragile and conflict-affected situations, PCR = project completion report, RRP = report and recommendation of the President, SIDS = small island developing states.

Objective

This guidance note describes and explains financial management and financial due diligence requirements in the context of fragile and conflict-affected situations, small island developing states, and emergency situations.

Living Document

This guidance note will be revised as needed. Various ADB policies and regulations (operations manual, project administration instructions) referred to in this guidance note are subject to revision from time to time. The reader is advised to consult the latest version of those documents.

The Reader

Readers are expected to use this guidance note to suit their needs. It is assumed that the reader is a professional with basic financial knowledge and involved in activities supported wholly or in part by ADB-financed or ADB-administered sovereign operations.

FAQs

Frequently asked questions, clarifications, examples, additional information, links to training, and other useful resources are available on the ADB website.

Legal Concerns and Order of Priority

Legal agreements govern the legal relationship between borrowers and ADB. If there is any discrepancy between this guidance note and legal agreements, the latter will prevail.

Acknowledgments

This guidance note was drafted by a team of dedicated and engaged staff in the Public Financial Management Division (PFFM) of the Procurement, Portfolio and Financial Management Department under the guidance of PFFM Director Srinivasan Janardanam. The core team comprised Tahmeen Ahmad (senior financial management specialist) and Aaron Pasquinel Cruz (associate financial management officer). Cecilia Peralta (senior financial management assistant) provided administrative support.

Copyediting was done by Terry Erle Clayton, proofreading by Levi Rodolfo Lusterio, cover design by Josef Ilumin, and layout by Edith Creus.

We acknowledge the pivotal guidance and support from the fragile and conflict-affected situations and small island developing states team in the Climate Change and Sustainable Development Department.

Valuable recommendations received during the interdepartmental review from the Sectors Group and ADB departments—Central and West Asia; Climate Change and Sustainable Development; East Asia; South Asia; Southeast Asia; Pacific; Strategy, Policy, and Partnerships; Independent Evaluation; Economic Research and Development Impact; Controllers; and Office of the General Counsel—significantly enriched the content and depth of the guidance note, and are gratefully acknowledged.

Abbreviations

ADB	–	Asian Development Bank
AEFS	–	audited entity financial statement
APFS	–	audited project financial statement
DMC	–	developing member country
FCAS	–	fragile and conflict-affected situations
FDD	–	financial due diligence
FMA	–	financial management assessment
FMS	–	financial management staff
FSA	–	FCAS and SIDS Approach
OM	–	operations manual
SIDS	–	small island developing states
TGN	–	technical guidance note

Executive Summary

Operating in fragile and conflict-affected situations (FCAS), small island developing states (SIDS), and emergency situations requires a deep understanding of unique country contexts, recognition of an elevated governance risk environment, adaptability to changing circumstances, and a long-term perspective for development impact.

Strategy 2030 of the Asian Development Bank (ADB) calls for differentiated approaches to development work in FCAS, SIDS, and subnational regions of poverty and fragility. The FCAS and SIDS Approach promotes the development and implementation of tailored approaches, cognizant of the specific contexts, drivers, and dimensions of fragility unique to each situation.

Financial management for ADB sovereign operations in FCAS and SIDS is grounded in ADB financial management guidance, derived from the ADB Charter, and aligned with the three core pillars of the FCAS and SIDS Approach: (i) improving responsiveness of standard ADB processes, procedures, and practices for FCAS and SIDS differentiated approaches; (ii) enhancing analytical tools and knowledge solutions to inform operations planning, design, and implementation; and (iii) building institutional capacity for operations in FCAS and SIDS.

Effective financial management arrangements for ADB sovereign projects rely upon the professional judgment of skilled and experienced financial management staff who balance fiduciary assurance with project and program implementation needs. In FCAS and SIDS with capacity constraints, a strategic approach focuses on long-term engagement, ongoing capacity enhancement, and governance improvement for sustainable impact rather than project-specific financial management arrangements as applied in larger countries or non-FCAS contexts.

This technical guidance note is also relevant for emergency situations and outlines process flexibility in financial management that may apply to FCAS, SIDS, and emergency situations. However, the list is not exhaustive, and further areas of flexibility may be identified and applied. The appendix provides examples of customized use of ADB's financial due diligence and management for ADB-financed sovereign projects in FCAS and SIDS, demonstrating best practices and potential challenges.

I. Introduction

1.1 This technical guidance note (TGN) outlines how to adapt the Asian Development Bank's (ADB) financial due diligence (FDD) and management requirements for ADB-financed sovereign projects in fragile and conflict-affected situations (FCAS), small island developing states (SIDS) contexts, and emergency situations. It recognizes the elevated risk environment in FCAS and SIDS, the chronic structural challenges faced by SIDS, and the rapidly evolving risk environments of emergency situations and recommends a differentiated approach. Flexibilities are incorporated without compromising ADB's fiduciary obligations.

1.2 In 2022, ADB classified 12 developing member countries (DMCs) as FCAS.[1] These DMCs are often impacted by weak governance and institutional capacity, economic and social insecurity, greater vulnerability to the effects of climate change and natural hazards, and, in some cases, political instability.[2] Situations of fragility tend to increase project financial management risks, persist for prolonged periods, and require continuous intervention. A conflict situation may require rapid interventions and flexibility to conduct FDD and monitoring activities remotely.

1.3 In 2022, 16 ADB DMCs self-identify as SIDS.[3] These DMCs are often characterized by structural vulnerabilities, including geographic remoteness and dispersion, small populations and markets, narrowly based economies, low fiscal revenue, and high import and export costs for goods. They are also susceptible to weak governance and institutional capacity, which can manifest in economic, social, and political instability. Many SIDS DMCs are among the most globally exposed countries to the impact of natural hazards and climate change.[4] The limited institutional capacity and vulnerability to external shocks elevate fiduciary risk in SIDS.

---

[1] A country is considered FCAS if it has an average rating of 3.2 or less based on the ADB country performance assessment and the World Bank Group country policy and institutional assessment.
[2] Asian Development Bank (ADB). 2016. *Mapping Fragile and Conflict-Affected Situations in Asia and the Pacific: The ADB Experience.* Manila.
[3] SIDS are recognized by the United Nations Office of the High Representative for the Least Developed Countries, Landlocked Developing Countries and Small Island Developing States (UN-OHRLLA). According to this, ADB recognized 16 of its DMCs as SIDS in 2022.
[4] ADB. 2021. *Fragile and Conflict-Affected Situations and Small Island Developing States Approach.* Manila.

1.4 Continuous capacity enhancement and robust engagement in governance and sustainability are the cornerstones of the financial management approach in FCAS and SIDS.

1.5 Emergency situations are threatening or realized conditions that require urgent action to avoid or address disruption and loss. This includes situations related to food, health, biological, industrial, and technological events.[5]

1.6 ADB borrowers and grant recipients need to work closely with ADB in determining suitable financial management arrangements in emergency situations, considering the financial management capacity of the executing and implementing agencies, country and sector context, preliminary risk assessment, urgency, support from other development partners, and all other factors that would contribute toward an effective emergency response.

A. ADB's Financial Management Architecture

1.7 ADB's financial management mandate derives from Article 14 of the ADB Charter, which requires ADB to pay due regard to whether the borrower and its guarantor can meet obligations under the loan; that ADB funds are used only for the purposes for which the loan was approved, with due attention to considerations of economy and efficiency; and that ADB operations are guided by sound banking principles.[6] The table summarizes ADB's publicly available financial management guidance materials during project processing and implementation, which also apply in FCAS, SIDS, and emergency situations.

Table: ADB Financial Management Guidance Materials

	Project processing	Project implementation
Operations Manual (OM)	• OM G2: Financial Due Diligence in Sovereign Operations	• OM J7: Financial Reporting, Auditing, Management, and Monitoring in Sovereign Operations
Technical Guidance Notes	• Cost Estimation for Sovereign Operations • Financial Analysis and Evaluation • Financial Due Diligence for Financial Intermediaries • Financial Management Assessment	• Financial Reporting and Auditing in Sovereign Operations

Source: Asian Development Bank.

---

[5] ADB. 2023. *Operations Manual OM D7 Disaster and Emergency Assistance*. Manila.
[6] ADB. 1966. *Agreement Establishing the Asian Development Bank*. Manila.

1.8 An illustration of ADB's financial management and due diligence requirements at each stage of the project cycle is depicted in Figure 1.

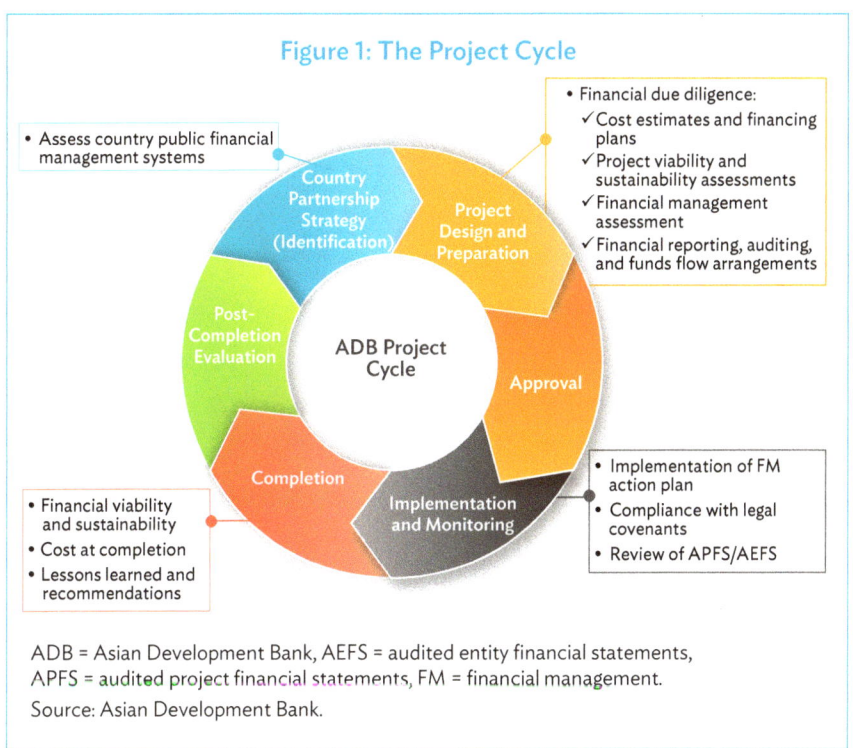

ADB = Asian Development Bank, AEFS = audited entity financial statements, APFS = audited project financial statements, FM = financial management.
Source: Asian Development Bank.

B. ADB's FCAS and SIDS Approach

1.9 ADB's Strategy 2030 calls for differentiated approaches to development work in FCAS, SIDS, and subnational regions of poverty and fragility.[7] Differentiated approaches, based on an understanding of the root causes, drivers, and dimensions of vulnerability, fragility, and conflict, and the multidimensional aspects of risk and resilience factors in the specific FCAS and SIDS contexts, are crucial to more productive ADB engagement with DMCs and improved development outcomes.

---

[7] ADB. 2018. *Strategy 2030: Achieving a Prosperous, Inclusive, Resilient, and Sustainable Asia and the Pacific*. Manila.

1.10 As a direct outcome of Strategy 2030, ADB published its FCAS and SIDS Approach (FSA) in June 2021.[8] The FSA outlines ADB's operational approach and action plan (2021–2025) for strengthening its development effectiveness in FCAS and SIDS. This action plan comprises 13 key action areas and 34 supporting sub-actions under three pillars (Figure 2). This FCAS, SIDS, and emergency situations TGN on financial management falls under the first pillar.

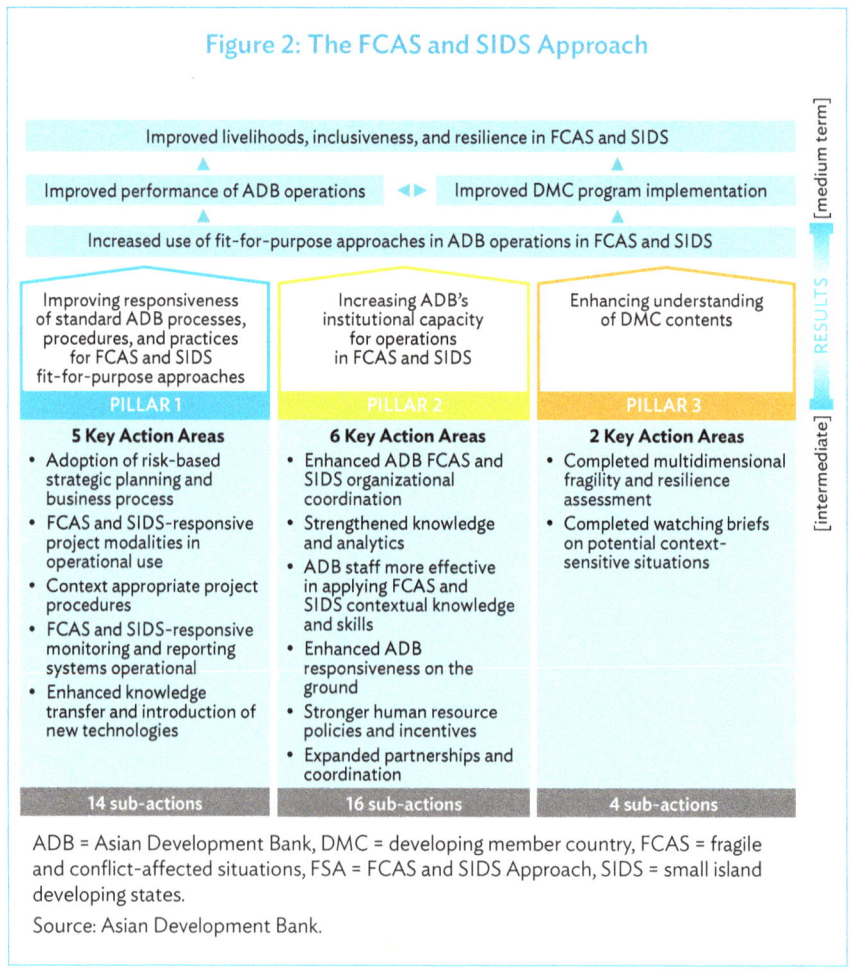

Figure 2: The FCAS and SIDS Approach

ADB = Asian Development Bank, DMC = developing member country, FCAS = fragile and conflict-affected situations, FSA = FCAS and SIDS Approach, SIDS = small island developing states.
Source: Asian Development Bank.

---

[8] Footnote 4.

II. Financial Management for FCAS, SIDS, and Emergency Situations

A. Differentiated Approaches

2.1 Financial management for ADB sovereign operations in FCAS and SIDS is based on the ADB financial management guidance (Table) and the three core pillars of the FSA. It is implemented with the dedicated support of qualified and experienced ADB financial management staff (FMS). While designing the financial management arrangements, the project FMS carefully balance the need for fiduciary assurance with an understanding of practical implementation constraints due to contextual factors. They also assess the need for capacity building and sustainable institutional strengthening.

2.2 The following broad principles are applied while operating in FCAS and SIDS contexts:

(i) **Context-specific approach.** No two FCAS or SIDS contexts are identical. This requires the design of tailored financial management arrangements that balance fiduciary assurance with practical implementation needs.

(ii) **Risk-based approach.** With inherent weaknesses in governance, the preliminary financial management risk is often substantial or high. The risk mitigation action plan considers the capacity of the executing and implementing agencies to mitigate financial management and financial sustainability risks.

(iii) **Sustained engagement.** Close monitoring of project financial management arrangements and sustained engagement for institutional strengthening is critical.

(iv) **Field presence and close coordination.** In-country presence and stakeholder coordination are essential for effective implementation support, especially when multiple development partners are involved. Fiduciary and financial management units serving multiple development partner-funded projects in a sector or country ensure continuity and reliability. ADB has also established several country offices in the Pacific region to improve interaction and deeper engagement with ADB's smallest DMCs.

B. Project Design and Due Diligence

2.3 ADB's project preparatory activities for sovereign operations include four FDD activities: the preparation of (i) financial management assessments (FMAs) of the executing and implementing agencies; (ii) cost estimates and a financing plan; (iii) financial analysis of the executing and implementing agencies, and where applicable, the financial evaluation of the project (or project components); and (iv) the design of fund flows, financial reporting, and auditing arrangements.

2.4 Financial management staff with the requisite skills, qualifications, and experience conduct FDD for ADB projects. These include experience in conducting due diligence in FCAS, SIDS, and emergency situations and the application of professional judgment to the project, agency, and country contexts.

2.5 The following sections summarize ADB's FDD requirements and discuss how these can be tailored to FCAS, SIDS, and emergency situations. The list is not exhaustive, and ADB financial management staff will work closely with the executing and implementing agencies to design bespoke financial management arrangements.

2.6 The appendix includes examples of tailored FDD activities in ADB-financed projects in FCAS and SIDS contexts.

Financial Management Assessment

2.7 **Overview.** An FMA evaluates the capacity evaluates the capacity of executing and implementing agencies for efficiently and effectively managing the financial resources for the proposed ADB programs and projects. The FMA is guided by ADB's OM G2: Financial Due Diligence in Sovereign Operations and TGN on FMA. The FMA draws on the country partnership strategy and its related governance risk assessment in establishing a robust financial management approach.[9]

2.8 Weak governance arrangements and capacity gaps heighten financial management risks in FCAS and SIDS. To address these risks, it is crucial to identify and transparently disclose all material financial management risks, allowing for mitigations in project financial management arrangements. In defining material PFM weaknesses and risks, it should be recognized that PFM and procurement systems in FCAS and SIDS may be less complex compared to other jurisdictions. What may be a material financial management risk in larger jurisdictions (such

---

[9] For the 12 small pacific island states (the PIC-12), the reference to country partnership strategy may be replaced by "the Pacific Approach."

as lack of accrual accounting or inadequate budget allocations for operations and maintenance of assets by key line ministries) might be a systemic and common finding in FCAS or SIDS contexts. Various aspects to be considered while tailoring the FMA are described as follows.

(i) **Flexibly managing evolving financial management risks.** Risks and opportunities continue to evolve and emerge during implementation. Financial management arrangements need to be sufficiently flexible to respond to shifting realities throughout implementation.

(ii) **Simplified financial management assessments.** When processing a project with an executing or implementing agency which has prior and recent experience with ADB, a simplified assessment may suffice, which will consist of an update to the agency's existing FMA.[10]

(iii) **Capacity building and supplementation.** Financial management capacity building is shaped by governance risk assessments, financial due diligence, best practices, and lessons learned from previous projects.[11] ADB crafts capacity enhancement plans for both the project and government, balancing institutional strengthening with capacity supplementation. Strengthening key public financial management institutions such as the central bank, the ministry of finance, and the supreme audit institution, as well as the finance teams of implementing and executing agencies, contributes to the achievement of sustainable development outcomes.

2.9 **Financial management assessment during emergency situations.** In emergency situations, efficient financial management is vital for a swift response and ensuring sufficient fund flows. Balancing immediate support with the recipient agency's ability to use, control, and report ADB funds is crucial. The FMA must be finalized before project approval and cannot be delayed. However, an existing FMA may be accepted during processing and updated within 3 months of approval if it is older than 2 years. For an FMA for new executing or implementing agencies, it should be completed during processing.

---

[10] The existing FMA should not be older than 2 years from the date of preparation.
[11] Tailored technical assistance programs can provide support, including on-the-job training, peer learning with other DMCs, and creating or updating financial management manuals. In SIDS contexts, where capacity is persistently low and staff turnover high, ADB may consider capacity supplementation through long-term consultancies and supporting financial management teams both at project and government level with appropriate funding. However, capacity supplementation is not without its own challenges, subject to funding risk, and offered for the short- to medium-term.

Cost Estimation

2.10 **Overview.** Cost estimates are prepared at the concept stage, refined throughout processing, updated during implementation, and validated at completion. The cost estimates cover the total cost to be incurred in delivering all outputs included in the project scope as defined in the legal agreement. Total project cost comprises base cost, contingencies, and financial charges during implementation. Cost-estimate preparation is guided by ADB's OM G2 and TGN on cost estimation in sovereign operations. To support high-quality cost estimates, project teams must ensure timeliness and realistic underlying assumptions.

2.11 **Challenges of cost estimation.** The likelihood of delays and cost overruns may be higher in FCAS and SIDS due to capacity constraints, limited experience, and general lack of administrative processes and oversight and—particularly for SIDS—remoteness and dispersion that can increase supply chain uncertainties and transportation costs.

2.12 **Financing project readiness.** ADB offers a project readiness facility for timely project preparation and reliable cost estimates. The Small Expenditure Financing Facility allows quick response to financing needs for small expenditures such as project preparation consultancies. Ongoing loans can include consulting packages for preparing feasibility studies, due diligence, and bidding documents for ensuing projects, enhancing the readiness for FCAS and SIDS projects.

2.13 **Refining cost estimates.** In areas with heightened uncertainty such as remote, inaccessible, or conflict-affected areas, as described in para. 2.11, contingency allocations may initially constitute a higher proportion of the cost estimates than usual. As additional information becomes available, cost estimates should be refined and updated both before project approval and during project implementation. This can reduce the risks of project delays, cost overruns, or loan cancellations.

2.14 **Cost estimation in emergency situations.** The cost estimates during emergency situations should follow the same principles for cost estimation as regular projects. During processing, the initial cost estimates may include a larger allocation for contingencies. Subsequently, ADB, working closely with executing and implementing agencies, can further refine cost estimates and reallocate contingencies to other line items to a level adequate for initiating procurement.

Financial Analysis and Evaluation

2.15 **Overview.** Financial analysis and evaluation of projects are two key steps in ADB's due diligence process for ensuring the prudent use of ADB's resources and identifying and mitigating risks to project and entity sustainability. Financial analysis and evaluation for ADB sovereign projects follow the guidance outlined in ADB's OM G2 and the TGN on Financial Analysis and Evaluation.

2.16 Financial analysis and evaluation for projects in FCAS and SIDS contexts follow the same methodology as in other situations. However, FCAS and SIDS contexts often face persistent systemic challenges that can harm sustainability. These challenges include limited government fiscal capacity, weak medium-term budget planning, absence of sector strategies and budget ceilings covering both capital and recurrent expenditures, supply chain issues impacting operations and maintenance costs, and a shortage of experienced staff. Project design in FCAS and SIDS should acknowledge such circumstances and develop mitigation measures for sustainability. Achieving financial sustainability in FCAS and SIDS contexts transcends projects and requires a sequenced, long-term approach, possibly involving a programmatic approach and technical assistance to address systemic issues.

2.17 **Designing financially sustainable projects.** Project design in FCAS and SIDS contexts should incorporate robust measures to optimize asset utilization and minimize the risk of premature deterioration, which can hinder the achievement of desired project outcomes. Some critical steps to mitigate risks and enhance the overall success and sustainability of projects include (i) ensuring adequate budget allocation and execution timeframe by the government, (ii) efficient budget utilization for asset maintenance, (iii) enhancing operational efficiency, (iv) strengthening entity governance, (v) early recruitment of operation and maintenance staff or consultants, and (vi) incorporating public–private partnership arrangements for the operation and maintenance of assets. Leveraging resources and involving the private sector can provide valuable support in optimizing asset usage and maintenance.

2.18 **Subsidizing tariffs for low-income households.** In FCAS and SIDS contexts, achieving full cost-recovery through tariffs, even for revenue-generating projects, may be challenging due to their impact on household incomes. A blend of sector regulation for cost-recovery tariffs, along with targeted subsidies and community service obligations for low-income households, can contribute equitably to the financial sustainability of ADB projects. Crucially, subsidies for vulnerable users should be funded by the government and not by the operating entity's income.

2.19 **Financial analysis and evaluation during emergency situations.** Preliminary financial analysis during processing may be limited to assurances from the DMC government to ensure prima facie sustainability. The detailed financial analysis can be deferred to the early stages of implementation but not later than 6 months from approval. Depending on the context, this assessment can include a historical and projected fiscal analysis of the executing agency, establishing its capacity to finance the running costs of project assets.

C. Project Implementation

2.20 **Overview.** Financial oversight during implementation involves ensuring the timely execution of the financial management action plan, compliance with legal covenants, and prompt financial reporting with independent audits to enhance accountability and provide verified financial data to stakeholders. ADB requires audited financial statements for all sovereign operations, including those in FCAS, SIDS, and emergency situations. This provides reasonable assurance that the proceeds of any loan made, guaranteed, or participated in by ADB, are used only for the purposes for which they were granted and comply with financial covenants incorporated in the legal agreements. Guidance is provided by ADB's OM J7: Project Financial Reporting, Auditing, Management, and Monitoring in Sovereign Operations, and the related TGN on Financial Reporting and Auditing in Sovereign Operations.

2.21 A decision to rely on country systems for project and financial management arrangements evaluates the DMC context, weighing the benefits of ring-fencing effective project implementation against the long-term objective of strengthening country systems and capacities. In FCAS context, gradually rebuilding financial management capacity in the line ministry can support projects and enhance public financial management. In SIDS, where capacity constraints exist for development projects, project implementation may be compelled to rely on ring-fenced project financial arrangements and external resources. The latter approach may also be more appropriate in emergency situations.

2.22 Working differently in FCAS, SIDS, and emergency situations can include one or a combination of the following measures:

Project and Financial Management Arrangements

(i) **Pooled project management.** In FCAS and SIDS contexts, a shortage of qualified financial management personnel is often a significant limitation. Instead of creating financial management units for each project, a centralized unit with a qualified and experienced FMS can provide consistent high-quality financial management support for all projects in a sector or DMC. This approach reduces the government's need to duplicate resources for each project. Long-term consultants, with relevant expertise and financed through loans or grants, can be deployed. Furthermore, development partners can consider shared service centers to enhance resource efficiency and consistency.[12]

(ii) **Financial management manuals.** Creating financial management manuals, developed in collaboration with agency staff familiar with

---

[12] A good practice example of project and financial management and monitoring is in the appendix.

local concerns, and providing ongoing capacity building for project financial management teams are essential components of project design. In DMCs with multiple development partners, harmonizing these manuals can ease the administrative workload for executing and implementing agencies.

(iii) **Alternative local delivery mechanisms.** In cases where central institutions are weak or impacted by conflict, financial management arrangements for project sites in remote locations may envisage alternative local delivery mechanisms, local control measures, and social accountability measures. In such an operating environment, ADB projects should support the development of distributed and remote financial management capacity.

(iv) **Alternative implementation arrangements.** ADB can partner with United Nations agencies or other development partners (e.g., civil society and nongovernment organizations), subject to appropriate FMAs. If found acceptable, ADB may also agree during the processing stage to adopt the financial management systems of such agencies for project implementation, reporting, and auditing. Third-party monitoring agencies may also be engaged to provide an additional layer of fiduciary assurance in such cases.

(v) **Transition arrangements in emergency situations.** Where ADB operations in a DMC with moderate to high financial management capacity are temporarily impacted (e.g., due to conflict, unrest, cross-border influx, natural hazards, or other emergencies), interim financial management arrangements may be put in place to ring-fence project financial management arrangements to compensate for the reduced capacity of the government agencies until normal systems are restored. Efforts should be made to transition back to country systems when the situation improves.

Fund Flows

(i) **Simplified disbursement arrangements.** Limiting the number of financing categories can allow flexibility in funds management, and allocating 100% financing of specific activities can avoid delays in counterpart funding.

(ii) **Managing fund flow risks.** In situations of heightened governance risks, weak financial management capacity, and limited agency pre-financing capability, direct payments can be considered for both large and small transactions. However, robust internal controls should be in place to approve these payments properly. When using advance accounts, requiring full documentation can mitigate the risk of unsubstantiated expenditures. Training the agency staff on submissions of withdrawal applications can help minimize errors and disbursement delays.

Accounting and Financial Reporting

(i) **Real-time computerized accounting.** The project may support the acquisition of customized computerized accounting and financial reporting software. By mandating the use of system-generated vouchers from the accounting software for releasing payments and ensuring prompt recording of third-party payments (such as ADB direct payments), the project can enhance the audit trail and maintain an up-to-date accounting system. This approach promotes the timely and accurate generation of financial reports, facilitating effective financial reporting practices.

(ii) **Simplified financial reporting.** To ensure effective oversight of project finances, it is beneficial to design and monitor financial reports that are frequent yet simplified. By updating expenditure information in real-time (e.g., ensuring transactions are paid only once inputted into the accounting management information system, based on system-generated invoices), key financial data can be readily incorporated into quarterly or biannual progress reports. Harmonizing project financial reporting formats with those of other development partners, whenever feasible, promotes consistency and facilitates collaboration.

(iii) **Disaster planning and resilience.** Create off-site backup sites for critical project financial data and systems, ensuring regular backup and maintenance plans to mitigate potential disruption risks.

Monitoring Mechanisms

(i) **Increased frequency of reviews.** Financial management desk reviews can be conducted more frequently based on a project's performance. Routine biannual or annual financial management review missions can be arranged, with special reviews addressing emerging major risks. Frequent meetings with project management and government agencies aim to identify and mitigate risks early.

(ii) **Social accountability mechanisms.** Monitoring is enhanced through appropriate agencies with strong accountability mechanisms and an established track record with other development partners. For example, when providing cash grants to beneficiaries, social audits and operational reviews by community groups and nongovernment organizations can promote accountability for the use of funds. Women-led collectives can be effective monitoring agents when beneficiaries are predominantly women.

(iii) **Leveraging technology.** When facing security risks or geographic limitations affecting field missions, technology can enhance monitoring. This includes virtual communication, mobile banking for small payments, and GIS tools for project data collection, analysis, and reporting, including tracking assets. Using big data analytics can also facilitate better supervision.

Auditing

(i) **Complementing limited external financial audit capacity.** Where supreme audit institutions lack the capacity to conduct project audits, ADB projects can finance the cost of private auditors. If agencies already have auditors, their audit scope can be amended to include new projects. In DMCs with limited audit capacity of the supreme audit institutions, this approach should be discussed at a DMC level.

(ii) **Exceptional extension of reporting deadlines.** Audited project financial statements (APFS) provide valuable, actionable information if submitted on time. Delayed submission undermines their utility. Enhancing agency and auditor capacity to submit audited financial reports on time is a preferable option to extending submission deadlines.[13] However, ADB may extend the due date for submission of APFS in exceptional cases.[14] To balance the risk, the financial management staff assigned to the project conducts alternate procedures to obtain assurance on the use of loan proceeds for intended purposes.[15]

(iii) **Special purpose audits.** In specific cases, an ADB loan or grant to an FCAS-classified country or SIDS may be used to finance a special purpose audit providing independent assurance on identified high or substantial financial management and governance risks identified during due diligence or to accommodate country requests to enhance the economy, efficiency, or effectiveness of specific government programs.[16]

---

[13] The submission deadline of APFS can be extended when there is (i) limited financial activity, (ii) low to moderate financial management risk, and (iii) the total reporting period is up to 24 months. In addition, project teams can seek guidance from the PPFD in exceptional circumstances that warrant an extension of the APFS submission deadline. ADB. 2022. *Financial Reporting and Auditing in Sovereign Operations: Technical Guidance Note*. Manila.

[14] For example, during the coronavirus disease (COVID-19) pandemic, ADB provided an extension of 6 months to the submission deadline, extended by a further 6 months for several SIDS, on their urgent request. ADB. 2020. *ADB's Comprehensive Response to the COVID-19 Pandemic*. Manila.

[15] The financial management action plan outlines alternative risk mitigation procedures, including increased frequency of financial management supervision missions and submission of unaudited quarterly or biannual project financial reports.

[16] To support the executing and implementing agencies, project cost estimates can provide for external audit fees, where audits are outsourced to private auditors, or the scope or frequency of audits is enhanced.

Appendix: Illustrative Examples from FCAS and SIDS Contexts

The following are practical illustrations from ADB fragile and conflict-affected situations (FCAS)-classified developing member countries (DMCs) and small island developing states (SIDS) sovereign operations. While some demonstrate good practice examples, there are also illustrations of pitfalls to avoid in these contexts.

Financial Management Assessment

Robust Asset Management Plans Contribute to Better Project Financial Management and Long-Term Sustainability

One finding in the project evaluations of the Independent Evaluation Department (IED) in the Pacific is the low sustainability of investments due to inadequate repairs and maintenance budgets.[1] Due diligence indicates no Asset Management Policy was available regarding maintenance of inventory of assets in the asset registers, the history of routine and major repairs, and how much funds are required. Such a policy can help the ministry prioritize the assets that would need maintenance and ensure they are operational throughout their useful lives.

Inadequate Financial Management Risk Mitigation Action Plans Can Impact Project Performance and Increase Integrity and Fiduciary Risks

In an FCAS country, no financial management risk action plan was prepared for a project with high financial management risk. This decreased the adequacy of financial management arrangements to ensure the use of loan proceeds for intended purposes. ADB's Office of Anticorruption and Integrity Project Procurement Related Review reported weak internal controls, inadequate records supporting eligible expenditures, and potential conflicts of interest. This impacted project implementation and increased exposure to integrity and fiduciary risks. IED's 2023 Annual Evaluation Review found that the effective design and monitoring of risk assessment and management plans contributed

---

[1] ADB. 2020. *2020 Annual Evaluation Review: ADB's Project Level Self-Evaluation System*. Manila.

to project success. In line with this, ADB's financial management function now closely monitors and reports on implementing the project's time-bound financial management risk mitigation plan.

Use of Statement of Expenditure Procedure Requires Adequate Agency Capacity, Close Monitoring, and Ongoing Risk Mitigation

The Statement of Expenditures Procedure is a simplified procedure to withdraw loan proceeds without submission of supporting documents. However, the project management unit (PMU) must keep complete documentation on file for future audits or spot-checking by ADB staff. The PMU did not maintain supporting records for transactions. ADB commissioned auditors to provide independent assurance on these transactions. The government was then asked to refund the amounts for which no supporting documentation was available. While the PMU continues to use the advance account after these shortcomings were identified, liquidation of advances now requires complete supporting documentation for all projects in the FCAS country involved. In addition, financial management and disbursement training for staff of PMUs in the country is being prioritized.

Working with UN Agencies in Conflict-Affected Situations Can Reduce Disruption to Project Processing and Implementation but Requires Tailored Financial Due Diligence to Identify and Address Financial Management Risks

In 2021, an unprecedented humanitarian crisis unfolded in a large FCAS DMC following political turmoil and upheaval. ADB, in coordination with other multilateral development banks, stepped in and started negotiations with four United Nations (UN) agencies to provide emergency support to the people for food security, health, and education.

Operating in this situation posed unique financial management challenges and risks associated with the project design, financial due diligence (FDD) requirements, and reputational matters. ADB engaged in extensive discussions with UN agencies on contextual challenges, i.e., restrictions on usual banking practices, the ban on women workers, and limitations imposed on the international community for contacting people. The following points summarize the tailored scope of financial due diligence, disbursement, and financial reporting and auditing arrangements for ADB's novel financing implemented by the UN agencies.

Financial due diligence:

- Standard cost estimates in the project approval documents were amended regarding the computation and presentation of contingencies.

- Financial analysis of the emergency assistance was waived.
- Disbursement procedures were tailored to the project. Specific templates were developed to facilitate the smooth implementation of projects. No ceiling on advance account utilization was set.
- The financial due diligence documents were not disclosed publicly.

Financial reporting and auditing:

- The UN single audit principle is applied at a project and entity level. Annual project financial statements, certified by the head of the country mission and controllers of relevant UN agencies were submitted to ADB. The UN agency submitted annual audited financial statements.

Monitoring financial management arrangements:

- ADB continues to closely monitor the developments in the country and prevalent financial management risks.

Cost Estimates

Utilizing the Project Readiness Facility Enhances Project Readiness and the Reliability of Cost Estimates

A project was planned to improve disaster resilience to cyclones, earthquakes, and associated tsunamis of a SIDS country by enhancing the breakwater of the port. With uncertainties on the depth of drilling in the seabed, over 30% of the project cost was allocated as physical contingencies during project preparation in October 2017. In July 2018, the project used a project design advance, now replaced by a project readiness facility (PRF), to conduct detailed technical due diligence with independent peer review, advance contracting for civil works, and update cost estimates based on the detailed technical design and procurement progress.[2] Using a PRF to enhance technical design significantly improved the reliability of cost estimates. The project was approved in August 2019. About 72% of total costs were allocated to specific cost categories in line with the procurement plan and physical contingencies were reduced to a reasonable level.

---

[2] A project design advance provides quick-disbursing of resources for project formulation, including detailed engineering design and broader project and program preparatory work (such as feasibility studies and due diligence, safeguard, and pre-implementation work). This was replaced by the project readiness financing modality in 2018.

Inadequate Technical Design Can Impact the Reliability of Cost Estimates and Result in Delays and Cost Overruns for Projects

Costs were estimated for a project to enhance the transmission and distribution network in a SIDS country considering the use of the "single-wire earth return system." During implementation, the proposed system was found to offer lower system resilience and safety features compared to alternative technologies such as the full three-phase system. This change to a better but higher-cost technology led to about 50% cost overruns, for which ADB processed additional financing.

Financial Analysis and Evaluation

Timely Maintenance Can Prevent Costly, Complex CAPEX Projects

Petroleum tank farm assets for power generation were no longer usable due to corrosion. The damage was attributable to the cancellation in 2012 of a $36,000 per annum maintenance contract for corrosion control. By 2019, corrosion threatened catastrophic failure of the tank farm and a $14 million project was approved by ADB for emergency rehabilitation.

Considering Financial Sustainability Risks during Project Design Can Improve Financial Sustainability

The project design reduced reliance on limited public funds for operation and maintenance in a SIDS country through several complementary measures: (i) establishing sound asset management practices, (ii) establishing a fund dedicated to regular operation and maintenance, (iii) regular tariff reviews, and (iv) involving nongovernment organizations for monitoring asset conditions.

Including Comprehensive, Tailored, and Complementary Measures at the Project Design Stage Can Improve Financial Sustainability

In 2020, ADB provided project and program financing for a balanced approach to energy sector reforms in a SIDS country. The project used the first financial intermediation loan for the country to improve access to clean energy loans for low-income households. A policy-based loan enhanced the corporate governance of the state-owned utility and strengthened its financial sustainability through cost-recovery tariff reforms.

Project and Financial Management and Monitoring

Centralized Project Management Facilities Can Supplement Limited Financial Management Capacity at a Sectoral or National Level

In 2012, the World Bank established a centralized fiduciary services unit in the ministry of finance of a SIDS country. The unit provides financial management, procurement, and other fiduciary services for projects in the DMC funded by the World Bank, ADB, the International Fund for Agricultural Development, and the United Nations Development Programme. The unit was staffed by long-term consultants who support ministries and supplement their project management capacity throughout project implementation for efficient and effective project delivery. In addition, the unit develops the financial management capacity of the DMC.

Financial Reporting and Auditing

A Systematic, Country Portfolio Assessment Can Help Identify and Address Reasons for Delays in Audited Financial Reporting to ADB

In a large, FCAS-classified country, ADB mobilized dedicated financial management experts to determine the cause of the delays in APFS submissions to ADB. The assessment began in 2019 and mapped processes and timelines of the financial reporting and audit cycle, including preparation of accounts by the project management unit, submissions to the supreme audit institution (SAI), allocations to private auditors, completion of an audit, and endorsement by the SAI. The assessment highlighted three bottlenecks that most contributed to the delays: (i) delays in appointing outsourced auditors by SAI, (ii) weak capacity of PMU accounting teams, and (iii) weak capacity of the SAI and timeliness of file review.

ADB engaged with the SAI to strengthen their understanding of ADB requirements and to develop and audit workflow highlighting key timelines and responsibilities. This plan was then communicated to the project teams and the outsourced auditors.

Due to these efforts, compliance significantly increased, and 83% of the projects for the FCAS country were submitted on time in 2020.

www.ingramcontent.com/pod-product-compliance
Lightning Source LLC
Chambersburg PA
CBHW040319170426
43197CB00022B/2971